Low-Carb Cookbook For Weight Loss

Follow the Effortless Guide For Weight Loss With Over 50
Low-Carb Recipes | Burn Fat and Reset Metabolism With
Tasty and Mouth-Watering Keto Recipes

Albert Lee

information. No warranties of any kind are declared or implied. Readers acknowledge that the author is not engaging in the rendering of legal, financial, medical or professional advice. The content within this book has been derived from various sources. Please consult a licensed professional before attempting any techniques outlined in this book.

By reading this document, the reader agrees that under no circumstances is the author responsible for any losses, direct or indirect, which are incurred as a result of the use of information contained within this document, including, but not limited to, errors, omissions, or inaccuracies.

Table of Contents

1. Chia And Blackberry Pudding

Serving: 2

Prep Time: 45 minutes

Cook Time: Nil

Ingredients

- ¼ cup chia seeds
- ½ cup blackberries, fresh
- 1 teaspoon liquid sweetener
- 1 cup coconut milk, full fat and unsweetened
- 1 teaspoon vanilla extract

How To

1. Take the vanilla ,liquid sweetener and coconut milk and add to blender

2. Process until thick

3. Add in blackberries and process until smooth

4. Divide the mixture between cups and chill for 30 minutes

5. Serve and enjoy!

Nutrition (Per Serving)

- Calories: 437
- Fat: 38g
- Carbohydrates: 8g
- Protein: 8g

2. Cinnamon Chiller

Serving: 1

Prep Time: 10 minutes

Ingredients:

- 1 cup unsweetened almond milk
- 2 tablespoons vanilla protein powder
- ½ teaspoon cinnamon
- ¼ teaspoon vanilla extract
- 1 tablespoon chia seeds
- 1 cup ice cubes

Directions:

1. Add listed ingredients to blender

2. Blend until you have a smooth and creamy texture

3. Serve chilled and enjoy!

Nutritional Contents:

- Calories: 145
- Fat: 4g
- Carbohydrates: 1.6g
- Protein: 0.6g

3. Cheesy Low-Carb Omelet

Serving: 5

Prep Time: 5 minutes

Cook Time: 5 minutes

Ingredients

- 2 whole eggs
- 1 tablespoon water
- 1 tablespoon butter
- 3 thin slices salami
- 5 fresh basil leaves
- 5 thin slices, fresh ripe tomatoes
- 2 ounces fresh mozarella cheese

- Salt and pepper as needed

How To

1. Take a small bowl and whisk in eggs and water

2. Take a non-stick Saute pan and place it over medium heat, add butter and let it melt

3. Pour egg mix and cook for 30 seconds

4. Spread salami slices on half of egg mix and top with cheese, tomatoes, basil slices

5. Season with salt and pepper according to your taste

6. Cook for 2 minutes and fold the egg with the empty half

7. Cover and cook on LOW for 1 minute

8. Serve and enjoy!

Nutrition (Per Serving)

- Calories: 451
- Fat: 36g
- Carbohydrates: 3g
- Protein:33g

4. Angel Eggs

Serving: 2

Prep Time: 30 minutes

Cook Time: Nil

Ingredients

- 4 eggs, hardboiled and peeled
- 1 tablespoon vanilla bean sweetener, sugar free
- 2 tablespoons Keto-Friendly mayonnaise
- 1/8 teaspoon cinnamon

How To

1. Halve the boiled eggs and scoop out the yolk

2. Place in a bowl

3. Add egg whites on a plate

4. Add sweetener, cinnamon, mayo to the egg yolks and mash them well

5. Transfer yolk mix to white halves

6. Serve and enjoy!

Nutrition (Per Serving)

- Calories: 184
- Fat: 15g
- Carbohydrates: 1g
- Protein: 12g

5. Roasted Onions And Green Beans

Serving: 6

Prep Time: 10 minutes

Cook Time: 15 minutes

Ingredients

- 1 yellow onion, sliced into rings
- ½ teaspoon onion powder
- 2 tablespoons coconut flour
- 1 and 1/3 pounds fresh green beans, trimmed and chopped
- ½ tablespoon salt

How To

1. Take a large bowl and mix salt with onion powder and coconut flour

2. Add onion rings

3. Mix well to coat

4. Spread the rings in the baking sheet, lined with parchment paper

5. Drizzled with some oil

6. Bake for 10 minutes at 400 Fahrenheit

7. Parboil the green beans for 3 to 5 minutes in the boiling water

8. Drain it and serve the beans with baked onion rings

9. Serve warm and enjoy!

Nutrition (Per Serving)

- Calories: 214
- Fat: 19.4g
- Carbohydrates:3.7g
- Protein: 8.3g

6. Denver Omelete

Serving: 1

Prep Time: 4 minutes

Cook Time: 1 minutes

Ingredients

- 2 tablespoons butter
- ¼ cup onion, chopped
- ¼ cup green bell pepper, diced
- ¼ cup grape tomatoes, halved
- 2 whole eggs
- ¼ cup ham, chopped

How To

1. Take a skillet and place it over medium heat

2. Add butter and wait until the butter melts

3. Add onion and bell pepper and Sauté for a few minutes

4. Take a bowl and whip eggs

5. Add the remaining ingredients and stir

6. Add Sautéed onion and pepper, stir

7. Microwave the egg mix for 1 minute

8. Serve hot!

Nutrition (Per Serving)

- Calories: 605
- Fat: 46g
- Carbohydrates: 6g
- Protein: 39g

7. Hungarian Keto Porridge

Serving: 2

Prep Time: 10 minutes

Cook Time: 5-10 minutes

Ingredients

- 1 tablespoon chia seeds
- 1 tablespoon ground flaxseed
- 1/3 cup coconut cream
- ½ cup water
- 1 teaspoon vanilla extract
- 1 tablespoon butter

How To

1. Add chia seeds, coconut cream, flaxseed, water and vanilla to a small pot

2. Stir and let it sit for 5 minutes

3. Add butter and place pot over low heat

4. Keep stirring as butter melts

5. Once porridge is hot/not boiling, pour into bowl

6. Enjoy!

7. Add a few berries or a dash of cream for extra flavor

Nutrition (Per Serving)

- Calories: 410
- Fat: 38g
- Carbohydrates: 10g
- Protein: 6g

8. Scrambled Pesto Eggs

Serving: 4

Prep Time: 5 minutes

Cook Time: 5 minutes

<u>Ingredients</u>

- 3 large whole eggs
- 1 tablespoon butter
- 1 tablespoon pesto
- 2 tablespoons creamed coconut milk
- Salt and pepper as needed

<u>How To</u>

1. Take a bowl and crack open your egg

2. Season with a pinch of salt and pepper

3. Pour eggs into a pan

4. Add butter and introduce heat

5. Cook on low heat and gently add pesto

6. Once the egg is cooked and scrambled, remove heat

7. Spoon in coconut cream and mix well

8. Turn on heat and cook on LOW for a while until you have a creamy texture

9. Serve and enjoy!

Nutrition (Per Serving)

- Calories: 467
- Fat: 41g
- Carbohydrates: 3g
- Protein: 20g

9. Vanilla Hemp Drink

Serving: 1

Prep Time: 10 minutes

Ingredients:

- 1 cup water
- 1 cup unsweetened hemp milk, vanilla
- 1 and ½ tablespoons coconut oil, unrefined
- ½ cup frozen blueberries, mixed
- 4 cup leafy greens, kale and spinach
- 1 tablespoons flaxseeds
- 1 tablespoons almond butter

Directions:

1. Add listed ingredients to blender

2. Blend until you have a smooth and creamy texture

3. Serve chilled and enjoy!

Nutritional Contents:

- Calories: 250
- Fat: 20g
- Carbohydrates: 10g
- Protein: 7g

10.   Pepperoni Omelet

Serving: 4

Prep Time: 5 minutes

Cook Time: 20 minutes

Ingredients

- 6 eggs
- 15 pepperoni slices
- 2 teaspoons coconut cream
- Salt and freshly ground black pepper , to taste
- 2 tablespoons butter

How To

1. Take a bowl and whisk eggs with all the remaining ingredients in it

2. Then take a skillet and heat butter

3. Pour the ¼ of egg mixture into your skillet

4. After that, cook for 2 minutes per side

5. Repeat to use the entire batter

6. Serve warm and enjoy!

Nutrition (Per Serving)

- Calories: 141
- Fat: 11.5g
- Carbohydrates: 0.6g
- Protein: 8.9g

11. The Mocha Shake

Serving: 1

Prep Time: 10 minutes

Ingredients:

- 1 cup whole milk
- 2 tablespoons cocoa powder
- 2 pack stevia
- 1 cup brewed coffee, chilled
- 1 tablespoon coconut oil

Directions:

1. Add listed ingredients to blender

2. Blend until you have a smooth and creamy texture

3. Serve chilled with some biscuits and muffins if you prefer, add Keto-Friendly whipped cream on top if desired

4. Enjoy!

Nutritional Contents:

- Calories: 293
- Fat: 23g
- Carbohydrates: 19g
- Protein: 10g

12. Early Morning Cheesy Egg Muffin

Serving: 6

Prep Time: 10 minutes

Cook Time: 20 minutes

Ingredients

- 4 large whole eggs
- 2 tablespoons Greek yogurt
- Salt and pepper taste
- 3 tablespoons coconut flour
- ¼ teaspoon baking powder
- ½ cup cheddar cheese, shredded

How To

1. Pre-heat your oven to 375-degree F

2. Add yogurt, eggs to a medium sized bowl

3. Season with salt and pepper, whisk well

4. Add baking powder, coconut flour and mix until you have a smooth batter

5. Add cheese and fold

6. Pour mix evenly in 6 silicone muffin cups and bake in your oven until golden

7. Enjoy!

<u>Nutrition (Per Serving)</u>

- Calories: 101
- Fat: 7g
- Carbohydrates: 3g
- Protein: 7g

13. An Omelet Of Swiss Chard

Serving: 4

Prep Time: 5 minutes

Cook Time: 5 minutes

Ingredients

- 4 eggs, lightly beaten
- 4 cups Swiss chard, sliced
- 2 tablespoons butter
- ½ teaspoon garlic salt
- Fresh pepper

How To

1. Take a non-stick frying pan and place it over medium-low heat

2. Once the butter melts, add Swiss chard and stir cook for 2 minutes

3. Pour egg into pan and gently stir them into Swiss chard

4. Season with garlic salt and pepper

5. Cook for 2 minutes

6. Serve and enjoy!

Nutrition (Per Serving)

- Calories: 260
- Fat: 21g
- Carbohydrates: 4g
- Protein: 14g

14. Chocolate Fat Bombs

Serving: 12 balls

Prep Time: 10 minutes + chill time

Cook Time: 5 minutes

<u>Ingredients</u>

- ¾ cup coconut oil
- 1 cup almond butter
- 1/3 cup cocoa powder
- ¼ cup almond, ground
- ½ teaspoon salt
- Stevia if needed

How To

1. Add listed ingredients to pot and place over low heat, stir until everything melts

2. Once the mixture is combined and forms a thick batter, let it cool

3. Roll mixture into balls and place on a paper lined baking tray

4. Place tray into fridge and let them cool for 1 hour

5. Serve and enjoy!

Nutrition (Per Serving)

- Calories: 555
- Fat: 55g
- Carbohydrates: 11g
- Protein: 11g

15. Coconut And Hazelnut Chilled Glass

Serving: 1

Prep Time: 10 minutes

Ingredients:

- ½ cup coconut milk
- ¼ cup hazelnuts, chopped
- 1 and ½ cups water
- 1 pack stevia

Directions:

1. Add listed ingredients to blender

2. Blend until you have a smooth and creamy texture

3. Serve chilled and enjoy!

Nutritional Contents:

- Calories: 457
- Fat: 46g
- Carbohydrates: 12g
- Protein: 7g

16. Delicious Nut Dredged Porridge

Serving: 4

Prep Time: 10 minutes

Cook Time: 15 minutes

Ingredients

- 1 cup cashew nuts, raw and unsalted
- 1 cup pecan, halved
- 2 tablespoons stevia
- 4 teaspoons coconut oil, melted
- 2 cups water

How To

1. Chop the nuts in food processor and form a smooth paste

2. Add water, oil, stevia to nuts paste and transfer the mix to a saucepan

3. Stir cook for 5 minutes on high heat

4. Lower heat to low and simmer for 10 minutes

5. Serve warm and enjoy!

Nutrition (Per Serving)

- Calories: 260
- Fat: 22g
- Carbohydrates: 12g
- Protein: 6g

17. Crispy Tofu

Serving: 8

Prep Time: 5 minutes

Cook Time: 20-30 minutes

Ingredients

- 1 pound extra firm tofu, drained and sliced
- 2 tablespoons olive oil
- 1 cup almond meal
- 1 tablespoons yeast
- ½ teaspoon onion powder
- ½ teaspoon garlic powder
- ½ teaspoon oregano
- ¼ teaspoon salt

How To

1. Add all ingredients except tofu and olive oil in a shallow bowl

2. Mix well

3. Pre-heat your oven to 400 degree F

4. In the wide bowl, add almond meal and mix well

5. Brush tofu with olive oil dip into the mix and coat well

6. Line a baking sheet with parchment paper

7. Transfer coated tofu to the baking sheet

8. Bake for 20-30 minutes, making sure to flip once until golden brown

9. Serve and enjoy!

Nutrition (Per Serving)

- Calories: 282
- Fat: 20g
- Carbohydrates: 9g
- Protein: 12g

18.Cottage Cheese Hotcake

Serving: 2

Prep Time: 10 minutes

Cook Time: 5-10 minutes

Ingredients

- 1 cup full –fat cottage cheese
- ½ cup full fat ricotta cheese
- 2 whole eggs
- ¼ cup coconut cream
- ½ teaspoon baking powder
- 1 teaspoon vanilla extract
- Butter for frying

- 2 teaspoon almond butter

How To

1. Add cottage cheese, ricotta cheese, eggs, coconut cream to a bowl, whisk well

2. Add ground almond, coconut flour, baking powder, vanilla extra and whisk until smooth

3. Take a non-stick frying pan and place it over medium heat

4. Add a knob of butter

5. Once butter melts, add dollops of batter onto hot pan

6. Once bubbles appear, flip the pancakes over

7. Serve with almond butter and some berries on top

8. Enjoy!

Nutrition (Per Serving)

- Calories: 690
- Fat: 48g
- Carbohydrates: 16g
- Protein: 40g

19.Choco Strawberry Keto Shake

Serving: 1

Prep Time: 10 minutes

Ingredients:

- ½ cup heavy cream, liquid
- 1 tablespoons cocoa powder
- 1 pack stevia
- ½ cup strawberry, sliced
- 1 tablespoons coconut flakes, unsweetened
- 1 and ½ cups water

Directions:

1. Add listed ingredients to blender

2. Blend until you have a smooth and creamy texture

3. Serve chilled with some Keto-Friendly whipped cream and berries on top

4. Enjoy!

Nutritional Contents:

- Calories: 470
- Fat: 46g
- Carbohydrates: 15g
- Protein: 4g

20. Mushroom Muffin

Serving: 12 muffins

Prep Time: 10 minutes

Cook Time: 15 minutes

Ingredients

- 3 cups mushrooms, sliced
- 1 medium-large zucchini, sliced
- 1 cup baby spinach leaves
- 5 eggs, lightly beaten
- Salt and pepper to taste
- 5 ounces cream cheese, broken into little pieces

How To

1. Pre-heat your oven to 375 degree F

2. Grease 12 hole-muffin tin

3. Place mushrooms, zucchini, spinach, eggs, salt and pepper to a bowl

4. Mix well

5. Pour mix into muffin pan and transfer to oven

6. Bake for 12-15 minutes

7. Make cream cheese frosting by stirring cream cheese to loosen it and bring to a spreadable consistency

8. Let the muffin cool and spread cream cheese

9. Enjoy!

Nutrition (Per Serving)

- Calories: 75
- Fat: 5g
- Carbohydrates: 2g
- Protein: 4g

21. Cinnamon And Coconut Porridge

Serving: 4

Prep Time: 5 minutes

Cook Time:5 minutes

Ingredients

- 2 cups water
- 1 cup 36% heavy cream
- ½ cup unsweetened dried coconut, shredded
- 2 tablespoons flaxseed meal
- 1 tablespoon butter
- 1 and ½ teaspoon stevia

- 1 teaspoon cinnamon
- Salt to taste
- Toppings as blueberries

How To

1. Add the listed ingredients to a small pot, mix well

2. Transfer pot to stove and place it over medium-low heat

3. Bring to mix to a slow boil

4. Stir well and remove the heat

5. Divide the mix into equal servings and let them sit for 10 minutes

6. Top with your desired toppings and enjoy!

Nutrition (Per Serving)

- Calories: 171
- Fat: 16g
- Carbohydrates: 6g
- Protein: 2g

22.   Skillet Based Kale And Avocado

Serving: 2

Prep Time: 5 minutes

Cook Time: 10 minutes

Ingredients

- 2 tablespoons olive oil, divided
- 2 cups mushrooms, sliced
- 5 ounces fresh kale, stemmed and sliced into ribbons
- 1 avocado, sliced
- 4 large eggs
- Salt and pepper as needed

How To

1. Take a large skillet and place it over medium heat

2. Add a tablespoon olive oil

3. Add mushrooms to pan and Saute for 3 minutes

4. Take a medium bowl and massage kale with remaining 1 tablespoon olive oil (for about 1-2 minutes)

5. Add kale to skillet and place them on top of mushrooms

6. Place slices of avocado on top of kale

7. Create 4 wells for eggs and crack each egg onto each hold

8. Season eggs with salt and pepper

9. Cover skillet and cook for 5 minutes

10. Serve hot!

Nutrition (Per Serving)

- Calories: 461
- Fat: 34g
- Carbohydrates: 6g
- Protein: 18g

23.   Fat Burner Espresso

Serving: 2

Prep Time: 10 minutes

Ingredients:

- 1 scoop Isopure Zero Carb protein powder
- 1 espresso shot
- ¼ cup Greek yogurt, full fat
- Liquid stevia, to sweeten
- Pinch of cinnamon
- 5 ice cubes

Directions:

1. Add listed ingredients to blender

2. Blend until you have a smooth and creamy texture

3. Serve chilled and enjoy!

Nutritional Contents:

- Calories: 270
- Fat: 16g
- Carbohydrates: 2g
- Protein: 30g

24.   Blue Cheese Omelet

Serving: 2

Prep Time: 10 minutes

Cook Time: 15 minutes

Ingredients

- 4 eggs
- Salt, to taste
- 1 tbsp sesame oil
- ½ cup blue cheese, crumbled
- 1 tomato, thinly sliced

How To

1. In a mixing bowl, beat the eggs and season with salt.

2. Set a saute pan over medium heat and warm the oil. Add in the eggs and cook as you swirl the eggs around the pan using a spatula.

3. Cook eggs until partially set.

4. Top with cheese; fold the omelet in half to enclose filling.

5. Decorate with tomato and serve while warm.

Nutrition (Per Serving)

- Calories: 307
- Fat: 25g
- Carbohydrates: 2.5g
- Protein: 18g

25.   Hearty Chia Bowls

Serving: 2

Prep Time: 10 minutes

Cook Time: Nil

<u>Ingredients</u>

- ¹/4 cup walnuts, chopped
- 1 and ¹/2 cups almond milk
- 2 tablespoons chia seeds
- 1 tablespoon stevia
- 1 teaspoon vanilla extract

How To

1. In a bowl, combine the almond milk with the chia seeds and the rest of the ingredients, toss, leave the mix aside for 10 minutes and serve for breakfast

Nutrition (Per Serving)

- Calories: 300
- Fat: 8g
- Carbohydrates: 5g
- Protein: 4g

26.   Classical Eggs And Canadian Bacon

Serving: 2

Prep Time: 10 minutes

Cook Time: 15 minutes

Ingredients

- 2 1-ounce slices of Canadian bacon
- 4 eggs
- 1/4 teaspoon ground black pepper
- Salt, to season
- 8 cherry tomatoes, halves

How To

1. Heat up a nonstick aluminum pan over a medium-high flame. Once hot, fry the bacon until crispy; reserve, living the rendered fat in the pan.

2. Turn the heat to medium-low.

3. Crack the eggs into the bacon grease. Cover the pan with a lid and fry the eggs until they are cooked through.

4. Salt and pepper to taste. Serve with the reserved bacon and cherry tomatoes on the side. Enjoy!

Nutrition (Per Serving)

- Calories: 326
- Fat: 5g
- Carbohydrates: 46g
- Protein: 0.7g

27.   Pecan And Goat Cheese

Serving: 4

Prep Time: 10 minutes

Cook Time: 10 minutes

<u>Ingredients</u>

- 1 lb log goat cheese
- 1/3 cup pecans, chopped
- 3 tablespoons bacon syrup
- 2 teaspoons fresh basil, chopped
- 1 teaspoon fresh chives, chopped

How To

1. In a small saucepan, add the chopped basil, bacon, and chives. Cook for 1-2 minutes and set aside.

2. Finely chop the pecans and transfer them to a large plate. Then roll the goat cheese in the chopped pecans.

3. Drizzle with the bacon mixture and serve. Enjoy

Nutrition (Per Serving)

- Calories: 296
- Fat: 8g
- Carbohydrates: 0.6g
- Protein: 14g

28.   Broccoli Egg Salad

Serving: 4

Prep Time: 10 minutes

Cook Time: Nil

Ingredients

- 1 pound broccoli florets, steamed
- 4 eggs, hard-boiled, peeled, and cut into wedges
- 2 spring onions, chopped'/2 teaspoon chili powder
- 1 tablespoon olive oil
- 1 tablespoon lime juice
- Salt and black pepper to the taste

How To

1. In a bowl, combine the broccoli with the eggs and the other ingredients, toss and serve for breakfast.

Nutrition (Per Serving)

- Calories: 250
- Fat: 11g
- Carbohydrates: 5.6g
- Protein: 6g

29.   Creamy Cheese Pancakes

Serving: 4

Prep Time: 10 minutes

Cook Time:12 minutes

<u>Ingredients</u>

- 2 organic eggs
- 2 ounces cream cheese, softened 1/2 teaspoon ground cinnamon 1 packet stevia
- Olive oil nonstick cooking spray

How To

1. Place all the ingredients in a blender and pulse until smooth.

2. Transfer the mixture into a bowl and set aside for about 2-3 minutes.

3. Grease a large nonstick skillet with cooking spray and heat over medium heat.

4. Add 1/4 of the mixture and tilt the pan to spread it in an even layer.

5. Cook for about 2 minutes or until golden brown.

6. Flip the side and cook for about 1 more minute.

7. Repeat with the remaining mixture.

8. Serve warm

Nutrition (Per Serving)

- Calories: 82
- Fat: 7.3g
- Carbohydrates: 0.8g
- Protein: 3.8g

30.   Excellent Zucchini Sage Cakes

Serving: 4

Prep Time: 10 minutes

Cook Time: 12 minutes

<u>Ingredients</u>

- 1 pound zucchinis, grated, and excess water drained
- Salt and black pepper to the taste
- 1 tablespoon almond flour
- 1 egg, whisked
- 1 tablespoon sage, chopped2 tablespoons olive oil

How To

1. In a bowl, combine the zucchinis with the flour and the other ingredients except for the oil, stir well and shape medium cakes out of this mix.
2. Heat up a pan with the oil over medium heat, add the cakes, cook them for 5-6 minutes on each side, drain excess grease on paper towels
3. Divide the cakes between plates and serve for breakfast

Nutrition (Per Serving)

- Calories: 320
- Fat: 13g
- Carbohydrates: 10g
- Protein: 12g

31. Delicious Egg Muffins

Serving: 4

Prep Time: 10 minutes

Cook Time: 20 minutes

<u>Ingredients</u>

- 6 tablespoons almond flour
- 2 tablespoons flaxseed meal
- 1/4 teaspoon baking soda
- 4 eggs
- 4 ounces cheddar cheese, shredded

How To

1. In a mixing bowl, thoroughly combine all of the above ingredients until well incorporated.
2. Line a muffin tin with non-stick baking cups. Scrape the batter into the prepared baking cups.
3. Bake in the preheated oven at 350 degrees F for 15 to 17 minutes.
4. Transfer to a wire rack to cool slightly before unmolding and serving. Bon appetit!

Nutrition (Per Serving)

- Calories: 292
- Fat: 5g
- Carbohydrates: 16g
- Protein: 3g

32.   Double Stuffed Cheese Peppers

Serving: 4

Prep Time: 10 minutes

Cook Time: 25 minutes

Ingredients

- 4 summer bell peppers, divined and halved
- 1 clove garlic, minced
- 4 ounces cream cheese
- 2 ounces mozzarella cheese, crumbled
- 2 tablespoons Greek-style yogurt

How To

1. Cook the peppers in boiling water in a Dutch oven until just tender or approximately 7 minutes.

71

2. Mix the garlic, cream cheese, mozzarella, and yogurt until well combined. Then, stuff the peppers with the cheese mixture.

3. Arrange the stuffed peppers on a til-lined baking pan.

4. Bake in the preheated oven at 360 degrees F for 10 to 12 minutes. Serve at room temperature.

Nutrition (Per Serving)

- Calories: 140
- Fat: 7g
- Carbohydrates: 8g
- Protein: 0.9g

33.   Creamy Cheese Muffins

Serving: 4

Prep Time: 10 minutes

Cook Time: 30 minutes

Ingredients

- 2 8-ounces packages of cream cheese
- 1/2 cup Erythritol
- 2 organic eggs
- 1/2 teaspoon organic vanilla extract
- 1 teaspoon ground cinnamon

How To

1. Preheat the oven to 350 degrees F. Grease 10 cups of a muffin tin.
2. In a bowl, add the cream cheese, Erythritol, eggs, and vanilla extract and beat until smooth.
3. Transfer mixture evenly into the prepared muffin cups and then sprinkle each with cinnamon.
4. Bake for about 20 minutes or until a wooden skewer inserted in the center comes out clean.
5. Remove the muffin tin from the oven and place it onto a wire rack to cool for about 10 minutes.
6. Carefully invert the muffins onto a wire rack to cool completely.
7. Serve

Nutrition (Per Serving)

- Calories: 344
- Fat: 33g
- Carbohydrates: 2.8g
- Protein: 9.1g

34.   Cheese And Bacon Balls

Serving: 4

Prep Time: 10 minutes + Chill time

Cook Time: 5 minutes

Ingredients

- 3 ounces bacon
- 6 ounces brie cheese
- 1 chili pepper, seeded and chopped
- 1/4 tsp parsley flakes
- 1/2 tsp paprika

How To

1. Set a pan over medium heat and fry the bacon until crispy; then crush it.
2. Place the other ingredients in a bowl and mix to combine with the bacon grease.
3. Refrigerate the mixture for 20 minutes.
4. Remove and form balls from the mixture. Set the bacon on a plate and roll the balls around to coat
5. Serve and enjoy!

Nutrition (Per Serving)

- Calories: 206
- Fat: 16g
- Carbohydrates: 0.6g
- Protein: 13g

35.   Baked Stuffed Up Avocados

Serving: 4

Prep Time: 10 minutes

Cook Time: 15-20 minutes

<u>Ingredients</u>

- 3 avocados, halved and pitted, skin on
- 1/2 cup mozzarella, shredded
- 1/2 cup Swiss cheese, grated
- 2 eggs, beaten
- 1 tbsp fresh basil, chopped

How To

1. Set oven to 360 F. Lay avocado halves in an ovenproof dish. In a bowl, mix both types of cheeses, pepper, eggs, and salt. Split the mixture
2. into the avocado halves. Bake for 15 to 17 minutes. Decorate with basil before Serves

Nutrition (Per Serving)

- Calories: 342
- Fat: 30g
- Carbohydrates: 8g
- Protein: 1g

36.   Colorful Vegetable Omelet

Serving: 4

Prep Time: 10 minutes

Cook Time: 5-10 minutes

Ingredients

- 2 tablespoons olive oil
- 1 cup Chanterelle mushrooms, chopped
- 2 bell peppers, chopped
- 1 white onion, chopped
- 6 eggs

How To

1. Heat the olive oil in a nonstick skillet over moderate heat. Now, cook the mushrooms, peppers, and onion until they have softened.

2. In a mixing bowl, whisk the eggs until frothy. Add the eggs to the skillet, reduce the heat to medium-low, and cook for approximately 5 minutes until the center starts to look dry. Do not overcook.

3. Taste and season with salt to taste.

Nutrition (Per Serving)

- Calories: 239
- Fat: 6g
- Carbohydrates: 11g
- Protein: 2g

37.   Simple Fried Eggs

Serving: 4

Prep Time: 10 minutes

Cook Time: 5-10 minutes

Ingredients

- 2 eggs
- 2 tbsp unsalted butter
- Seasoning:
- 1/4 tsp salt
- 1/8 tsp ground black pepper

How To

1. Take a skillet pan, place it over medium heat, add butter and when it has melted, crack eggs in the pan.

2. Cook eggs for 3 to 5 minutes until fried to the desired level, then transfer the eggs to serving plates and sprinkle with salt and black pepper.

3. Serve.

Nutrition (Per Serving)

- Calories: 179
- Fat: 16g
- Carbohydrates: 0.5g
- Protein: 8g

38. Beef And Egg Early Morning Muffin

Serving: 12

Prep Time: 10 minutes

Cook Time: 15 minutes

Ingredients

- 2 lbs of ground beef (20% fat/80% lean meat ratio)
- 1 tbsp of mixed herbs
- 12 eggs
- 1 cup of shredded cheddar cheese
- 2 and 1/2cups of spinach

How To

1. In a deep pan, saute the spinach with some olive oil for a few minutes until wilted. Remove from the heat and set aside.

2. In a 12-piece muffin, a tin dish begins lining each tin with around 1-2 tbsp of the ground beef to make a base cup. You should cover all sides of the tin and leave room for the spinach and eggs.

3. Top each meat cup with spinach, cheese, and one egg on top.

4. Cook in the oven for 15-18 minutes at 400F/200C

Nutrition (Per Serving)

- Calories: 222
- Fat: 18g
- Carbohydrates: 1.2g
- Protein: 15.2g

39.   Spicy Chili Deviled Eggs

Serving: 4

Prep Time: 10 minutes

Cook Time: 50 minutes

<u>Ingredients</u>

- 1/4 of lime, juiced
- 2 eggs, boiled
- 2 tsp chili garlic sauce
- 1/2 tsp paprika
- 1/8 tsp ground black pepper

How To

1. Peel the boiled eggs, then slice in half lengthwise and transfer egg yolks to a medium bowl by using a spoon.
2. Mash the egg yolk, add remaining ingredients and stir until well combined.
3. Spoon the egg yolk mixture into egg whites and then serve.

Nutrition (Per Serving)

- Calories: 82
- Fat: 5g
- Carbohydrates: 0.4g
- Protein: 7g

40.   Classic Egg Porridge

Serving: 4

Prep Time: 10 minutes

Cook Time: 15 minutes

Ingredients

- 2 organic free-range eggs
- 1 / 3 cup organic heavy cream without food additives
- 2 packages of your preferred sweetener
- 2 tbsp grass-fed butter ground organic cinnamon to taste

How To

1. In a bowl, add the eggs, cream, and sweetener, and mix together.
2. Melt the butter in a saucepan over medium heat. Lower the heat once the butter is melted.
3. Combine together with the egg and cream mixture.
4. While Cooking, mix until it thickens and curdles.
5. When you see the first signs of curdling, remove the saucepan immediately from the heat.
6. Pour the porridge into a bowl. Sprinkle cinnamon on top and serve immediately.

Nutrition (Per Serving)

- Calories: 604
- Fat: 45g
- Carbohydrates: 2g
- Protein: 8g

41.Juicy Spanish Omelet

Serving: 4

Prep Time: 10 minutes

Cook Time: 10 minutes

Ingredients

- 3 eggs
- Cayenne or black pepper
- 1/2 cup finely chopped vegetables of your choosing.

How To

1. In a pan on high heat, stir-fry the vegetables in extra virgin olive oil until lightly crispy.
2. Cook the eggs with one tablespoon of water and a pinch of pepper.
3. When almost cooked, top with the vegetables and flip to cook briefly.
4. Serve

Nutrition (Per Serving)

- Calories: 160
- Fat: 15g
- Carbohydrates: 4g
- Protein: 7g

42.   Delicious Breakfast Sausage Casserole

Serving: 4

Prep Time: 10 minutes

Cook Time: 45 minutes

Ingredients

- 8 eggs, beaten
- 1 head chopped cauliflower
- 1 lb sausage, cooked and crumbled
- 2 cups heavy whipping cream
- 1 cup sharp cheddar cheese, grated

How To

1. Cook the sausage as usual.

2. In a large bowl, mix the sausage, heavy whipping cream, chopped cauliflower, cheese, and eggs.

3. Pour into a greased casserole dish.

4. Cook for 45 minutes at 350°F/175°C, or until firm.

5. Top with cheese and serve.

Nutrition (Per Serving)

- Calories: 290
- Fat: 25g
- Carbohydrates: 1g
- Protein: 12g

43.   Excellent Scrambled Mug Eggs

Serving: 4

Prep Time: 10 minutes

Cook Time: 5 minutes

Ingredients

- 1 mug
- 2 eggs
- Salt and pepper
- Shredded cheese
- Your favorite buffalo wing sauce

How To

1. Crack the eggs into a mug and whisk until blended.

2. Put the mug into your microwave and cook for 1.5 - 2 minutes, depending on the power of your microwave.
3. Leave for a few minutes and remove from the microwave.
4. Sprinkle with salt and pepper. Add your desired amount of cheese on top.
5. Using a fork, mix everything together.
6. Then add your favorite buffalo or hot sauce and mix again.
7. Serve!

Nutrition (Per Serving)

- Calories: 330
- Fat: 30g
- Carbohydrates: 1g
- Protein: 12g

44.   Unique Salmon Omelet

Serving: 4

Prep Time: 10 minutes

Cook Time: 5-10 minutes

<u>Ingredients</u>

- 3 eggs
- 1 smoked salmon
- 3 links beef sausage
- 1/4 cup onions
- 1/4 cup provolone cheese

How To

1. Whisk the eggs and pour them into a skillet.
2. Follow the standard method for making an omelet.
3. Add the onions, salmon, and cheese before turning the omelet over.
4. Sprinkle the omelet with cheese and serve with the sausages on the side.
5. Serve!

Nutrition (Per Serving)

- Calories: 460
- Fat: 35g
- Carbohydrates: 2g
- Protein: 36g

45.   Fine Spinach And Cheese Eggs

Serving: 4

Prep Time: 10 minutes

Cook Time: 25-30 minutes

Ingredients

- 3 whole eggs
- 3 oz cottage cheese
- 3-4 oz chopped spinach 1/4 cup parmesan cheese 1/4 cup of milk

How To

1. Preheat your oven to 375°F/190°C.
2. In a large bowl, whisk the eggs, cottage cheese, parmesan, and milk.

3. Mix in the spinach.

4. Transfer to a small, greased oven dish.

5. Sprinkle the cheese on top.

6. Bake for 25-30 minutes.

7. Let cool for 5 minutes and serve.

8. Serve!

Nutrition (Per Serving)

- Calories: 200
- Fat: 25g
- Carbohydrates: 2g
- Protein: 16g

46.   Juicy Scotch Egg

Serving: 4

Prep Time: 10 minutes

Cook Time: 25-30 minutes

Ingredients

- 4 large eggs
- 1 package beef Sausage (12 oz)
- 8 slices thick-cut beef bacon
- 4 toothpicks

How To

1. Hard-boil the eggs, peel the shells, and let them cool.

2. Slice the sausage into four parts and place each part into a large circle.
3. Put an egg into each circle and wrap it in the sausage.
4. Place inside your refrigerator for 1 hour.
5. Make a cross with two pieces of thick-cut bacon.
6. Place a wrapped egg in the center, fold the bacon over the top of the egg and secure with a toothpick.
7. Cook inside your oven at 450°F/230°C for 25 minutes.
8. Enjoy!

Nutrition (Per Serving)

- Calories: 345
- Fat: 28g
- Carbohydrates: 2g
- Protein: 18g

47. Toasty Cauliflower And Avocado

Serving: 4

Prep Time: 10 minutes

Cook Time: 5-10 minutes

Ingredients

- 1 large egg
- 1 grated cauliflower head
- 1 chopped avocado
- 3/4 cup shredded mozzarella cheese
- Salt &Black pepper

How To

1. Set the oven to preheat at 420 F, then line the baking tray with a parchment paper
2. Cook the cauliflower in the microwave on high for 7 minutes
3. Allow the cauliflower to cool, then drain on a paper towel.
4. Remove the excess moisture by pressing with a clean kitchen towel, then put them in a bowl.
5. Add the egg and mozzarella, then stir
6. Add the seasonings and mix evenly, then shape the mixture into medium squares
7. Arrange the squares on the prepared baking tray.
8. Allow baking until browned evenly, for about 20 minutes
9. In the meantime, puree the avocado with black pepper and salt.
10. Top with the pureed avocado.
11. Serve!

Nutrition (Per Serving)

- Calories: 126
- Fat: 7g
- Carbohydrates: 10g
- Protein: 10g

48.   Avocado Egg Crepes

Serving: 4

Prep Time: 10 minutes

Cook Time: 5 minutes

Ingredients

- 4 eggs
- 3/4 sliced avocado
- 2 teaspoons olive oil
- 1/2 cup alfalfa sprouts
- 4 slices shredded turkey breast

How To

1. Pour the olive oil into a pan and heat over medium heat

2. Crush the eggs and cook for 3 minutes on each side of the pan as you spread to cook evenly.

3. Remove the eggs from heat, then top with avocado, turkey breast, sprouts, and alfalfa, then roll up well.

4. Serve!

Nutrition (Per Serving)

- Calories: 371
- Fat: 25g
- Carbohydrates: 10g
- Protein: 27g

49.   Bacon And Shallots With Spinach

Serving: 4

Prep Time: 10 minutes

Cook Time: 20-25 minutes

Ingredients

- 16 oz raw spinach
- 1/2 cup chopped white onion
- 1/2 cup chopped shallot
- 1/2 pound raw bacon slices
- 2 tbsp butter

How To

1. Slice the bacon strips into small narrow pieces.

2. In a skillet, heat the butter and add the chopped onion, shallots, and bacon.

3. Saute for 15-20 minutes or until the onions start to caramelize and the bacon is cooked.

4. Add the spinach and saute on medium heat. Stir frequently to ensure the leaves touch the skillet while cooking.

5. Cover and steam for around 5 minutes, stir and continue until wilted.

6. Serve!

Nutrition (Per Serving)

- Calories: 150
- Fat: 13g
- Carbohydrates: 5g
- Protein: 4g

51. The Cheesy Mug

Serving: 1

Prep Time: 4 minutes

Cook Time: 1-2 minutes

<u>Ingredients</u>

- 2 ounces roast beef slices
- 1 and ½ tablespoons green chilies, diced
- 1 and ½ ounces pepper jack cheese, shredded
- 1 tablespoon sour cream

How To

1. Layer roast beef on the bottom of your mug, making sure to break it down into small pieces

2. Add half a tablespoon of sour cream, add half tablespoon green Chile and half an ounce of pepper jack cheese

3. Keep layering until all ingredients are used

4. Microwave for 2 minutes

5. Server warm and enjoy!

Nutrition (Per Serving)

- Calories: 268
- Fat: 16g
- Carbohydrates: 4g
- Protein: 22g